The Rhythm of Truth

BY

HARIDAS CHAUDHURI

Professor of Philosophy and Religion
and Chairman of the Department of South Asia,
The American Academy of Asian Studies,
San Francisco

With a Foreword by

ERNEST WOOD

President and Dean of The American Academy
of Asian Studies

CULTURAL INTEGRATION FELLOWSHIP

SAN FRANCISCO

HARIDAS CHAUDHURI

To
WALTER S. JOHNSON

Whose living faith in the supreme creator
Has been a factor in constructive living.

BOOKS BY HARIDAS CHAUDHURI

The Philosophy of Integralism

Sri Aurobindo: The Prophet of Life Divine

Prayers of Affirmation (A Guide to Daily Meditation)

The Rhythm of Truth

Indian Culture (co-editor)

The Integral Philosophy of Sri Aurobindo (co-editor)

MĀ or The Mother (in Bengali)

Sri Aurobinder Sādhanā (in Bengali)

Contents

Foreword

What is the nature of Truth? The author of this volume, which contains the wisdom of ancient sages recast in a novel form, puts his finger immediately and unerringly upon the answer by saying that it is knowledge of reality as the interplay of unity and diversity. That which exists in its own right, not depending on anything else for its being, is the real. The real is the royal, the kingly, which as such is above all laws and influence, and is the summum genus of all categories and the substance of all being. As such it is present everywhere and at all times. The author, Dr. Haridas Chaudhuri, who is a brilliant exponent of the concept of truth as creative harmony, points out that each kind of human experience and sentiment, every item of our world of known things and inner feelings, discloses the intermingling of the one and the many in the concrete texture of reality. Unity and diversity never clash; the advancing discoveries of natural law in the field of science constitute an increasing perception of that harmony, and human progress is our expanding application of it, whether in individual character or in social cooperation, whether in act, in feeling, or in thought.

Dr. Chaudhuri has applied the main principle to a variety of human ideals, showing the way to human fulfillment and balanced integration, but he has done more than this by presenting it in poetic form in a variety of ways. There is in this, not only every now and then, an exquisite touch of picturization, but also that effect of poetry which creates a pause in consciousness inducing a moment's changeless dwelling on the presented experience or the focalized truth. The variety of poetic form in these poems is very feelingly adapted to the various topics such as "The Secret of Meditation" where the last two lines in each verse set the seal upon its contents, and in "Self-Offering" where one thing after another in ordered process is laid upon the altar of dedication. These poems will yield rich fruit to those who read them with a spiritual opening to the light of truth.

This little volume may also cause its Western readers to realize that the frequently presented idea that Eastern and especially Indian aspiration is bent upon retirement from the world and, in the extreme, individual withdrawal from life, is wrong. It will show, on the contrary, that the ideal is withdrawal from folly and selfishness and from dogmatic or dualistic thinking, whereby the practice of harmony in act, in feeling and in thought, will lead to the direct experience of that creative unity in which lies not mere peace but happiness beyond all description and understanding.

ERNEST WOOD

San Francisco,
August 14, 1958

Preface

Truth in its inmost essence is beyond all forms and images, beyond all dogmas and creeds, beyond all imperfect conceptual formulations. But truth in its dynamic expression has multitudinous forms and aspects, levels and degrees, images and symbols. Every individual or group has its own unique way of mirroring the light of truth. Every inward apprehension of truth, every thought system or cultural pattern, has its own unique rhythm, which expresses itself in characteristic thoughts, words, actions, emotional reactions, etc. Unique rhythm is indeed an essential ingredient of the outward expression of truth.

Verses contained in the following pages are an imperfect attempt to express the rhythm of some of the author's insights into the nature of truth. If any reader finds any help here in his or her own quest of truth, the labor of the author will be amply rewarded. The verses are preceded by a brief statement of the integral conception of truth as creative harmony. Truth conceived as creative harmony gives a profound meaning to our life, a divine significance to the world process, and a dynamic importance to the different religious and philosophical ideas of man.

I wish to take this opportunity of offering my grateful thanks to Professor Ernest Wood, President and Dean of the American Academy of Asian Studies, for his valuable suggestions and for his kindly contributing a Foreword. My sincere thanks are also due to all those who have helped me in various ways in bringing out this volume including my wife Bina and our esteemed friend Bertha Francesconi.

HARIDAS CHAUDHURI

San Francisco,
August 15, 1958

The Nature of Truth

"Truth is one, sages call it by different names,"[*] declared the ancient sages. Unity in diversity, diversity in unity,—that is indeed the standing miracle of existence. Endless variations mark the ceaseless flow of creation, but underlying them all there is one cosmic principle of creative unity. That unity is perpetually productive of the many, because it is infinitely rich in content. Essentially beyond all forms and images, it is multiform and multi-colored in manifestation. It is the one Light that shines in various forms. The great religions of the world have tried to identify that creative One or cosmic Light by various names. Judaism calls it Jehovah, Christianity calls it God, Islam calls it Allah, Zoroastrianism calls it Ahura Mazda, Hinduism calls it Brahman, Buddhism calls it Sunyata, Taoism calls it Tao, and so on. All these different names, which are the central concepts in different religious systems of the world, are varying modes of apprehension and designation of the one universal Truth which is the common substratum of all religions.

Again it is the same universal Truth which different philosophies of the world try to articulate in intellectual terms in different ways. Some philosophers call it Matter or Energy, some call it Life Force, some call it cosmic Mind, some call it ineffable Spirit, some call it the Unknown and Unknowable, some call it the Void or Silence, and so on. Since Truth is infinite, no philosophy can exhaustively express it. No philosopher can truthfully declare that he is uttering the last word and that nothing more can be said about it. There can be no such thing as finality in the sphere of knowledge.

---

[*] Rig Veda, x 14.

Dogmatism is incompatible with the spirit of wisdom. But just as no philosophic system is absolutely true, none is absolutely false either. Every philosophic system has a certain value and importance of its own insofar as it tries to express the nature of reality under certain conditions, serving a special purpose of human evolution. Every thought system beholds the Truth from a certain standpoint or perspective, and provides a special formulation which is relatively valid and useful. Thus we may say that apparently conflicting philosophical systems of the world are in essence different modes of logical articulation or verbalized expression, relatively valid and useful, of the one supreme Truth.

An understanding of the multiform richness of the one infinite Truth makes one realize the fundamental unity of all religions and of all philosophies. It makes one realize that the apparently divergent religions of the world are different forms of manifestation under different historical conditions of one eternal religion. That eternal religion is the law of living in harmony with the Infinite. It is also important to realize that the seemingly conflicting thought systems of the world are different forms of manifestation in the medium of human thinking of one perennial philosophy. That perennial philosophy is the all-comprehending supra-intellectual vision of the total truth. It is the self-awareness of the Infinite expressing itself in endlessly various forms.

Truth and Other Values

When we consider truth in its most comprehensive sense apart from all subjective apprehension of the human mind, we call it Reality. Reality is the totality of existence; it is the fullness of being. The nature of reality as disclosed to human understanding is truth (*satya*) in its human actuality. The nature of reality or the essence of truth as reflected in man's emotional expression is beauty (*sundara*) as an actualized value. The nature of reality as reflected in man's actions and social relations is goodness (*shiva*) as an actualized value. Truth, beauty and goodness are inseparable aspects or modes of manifestation of the same reality. Truth is the ideal of self-fulfillment of man's intellectual nature. Beauty is the ideal of self-fulfillment of man's emotional nature. Goodness is the ideal of self-fulfillment of man's active or volitional nature. Since truth in its transcendental essence is not different from reality, we may say that reality is absolute truth. But absolute truth is no determinate idea, no fixed doctrine, no unalterable thought-structure—it is the self-transcendence of all ideas and theories in the indeterminable essence of reality. Likewise, since beauty in its transcendental essence is not different from reality, we may say that reality is absolute beauty. But absolute beauty is no particular style of art expression, no determinate and unalterably fixed aesthetic standard, but the self-transcendence of all specific aesthetic styles and criteria in the unfathomable depth of reality. Similarly, goodness in its transcendental essence is reality, so that we may say reality is absolute goodness. But absolute goodness is no particular moral code or ethical system of any particular country or historical epoch,—it is the self-transcendence of all ethical systems in the dynamic law of self-expression of reality. This is why such words as reality, truth, beauty, goodness, etc. imperceptibly shade off into one another, giving rise to very subtle nuances of meaning in different contexts of human speech. They are in essence identical, and yet distinct in expression. They have each a distinguishable form, but yet they are inseparable in being.

When we understand that reality is beyond all particular forms and images, beyond all fixed ideas and theories, beyond all actualized values and determinate expressions, we experience it as full freedom. This experience broadens the mental horizon and liberates the soul. It emancipates man from all emotional ties and the fetters of the ego. Love is the spontaneous outflow of such inner freedom. It is the joyful self-relating of one soul to another. It is the spirit of fellowship in the common enterprise of life. It is the emotional expression of the realization of unity and freedom. It is unmotivated selfless action,—action that conquers the challenge of the not-self. Now, we are in a position to sum up by saying: reality is full freedom in its inmost essence; it is the unity of truth, beauty and goodness in its relation to human personality; it is love in its expression in the sphere of the many or in interpersonal relations.

The Truth About Individuality

We have seen that reality in its inmost essence is freedom, absolute freedom. Absolute freedom implies infinite creativity. Since the supreme spirit is absolutely free, it is capable of creating endless forms, without being limited by any or all of them. It is the cosmic creative principle, the all-originating life-force, the all-sustaining center, the all-fulfilling value. It is the beginning and the middle and the end of creation. It is the first cause and the inner controller and the animating goal of the world process. This universal creative principle, out of the fullness of its creative joy, differentiates itself into an endless plurality of individual selves. Every individual self is in essence a creative center of self-expression of the supreme spirit. It is a unique mode of manifestation of the universal, a spark of the cosmic flame. So long as the individual lives in utter self-forgetfulness of his true nature, he suffers. He considers himself a self-contained atomic entity, separate from the universal source and also separate from other individuals. Thus he imprisons himself within the stone walls of his own making. Wisdom begins with the pulling down of such stone walls of ego-centric existence. It matures with an increasing insight into the true nature of one's own self as a creative center of the cosmic whole. It is consummated with the individual actively fulfilling his unique creative role in the drama of life as a channel of activity of the supreme spirit.

The External World

What is the truth about the external world? How is the phenomenal universe related to the supreme creator? There are some who consider the external material world to be ultimately real and to be the only reality. In their view the material universe is self-creating and self-sustaining, and as such does not need any divine creator. They are materialists or naturalists. In their eagerness to vindicate the reality of matter and the laws of nature, they turn a blind eye to the higher spiritual values of life. There are some again who think that the material world is created and governed by a transcendental Deity who rules it from above. This is popular theism. In its eagerness to exalt God to the rank of the Most High it makes God actually finite, because, in their conception, God is limited by the existence of the whole material universe outside of Him. Then again there are some who consider the external world unreal, or at best only conventionally real, but illusory in the ultimate reference. This is called illusionism or acosmism. In its eagerness to affirm the absolute reality of spiritual values, it takes up a negative attitude to our life in the material world and robs it of ultimate significance.

Truth which is all-inclusive harmony reconciles all one-sided extremes. It is the balanced view of the totality of existence. It is the synoptic vision of reality in its concrete fullness. The material world is not ultimately real, existing by itself, standing on its own bottom. Nor is it unreal and void of ultimate significance. Nor is it all matter, radically opposed to, and existing outside of, an all-ethereal being called God. It is an infinitely variegated form of manifestation of the supreme Spirit. It springs from the depths of one cosmic consciousness which encompasses it and penetrates it through and through. It exists in the medium of one cosmic intelligence which endows it with profound significance. The world is real, because it is the manifestation of that which is the source of all reality. It is not a passing shadow-show. Nor is it "a tale told by an idiot full of sound and fury and signifying nothing." The world is significant, because it is the sphere of expression of the higher values of life. The element of unreality in the world comes from our distorted perception of it. It is due to the colored glasses that we wear,—the glasses made of our warped emotions and ego-centric desires. The spiritual destiny of life is to discard such colored glasses, to enjoy the right perspective of things as they are, and to participate with full affirmation in the festival of divine delight that life is.

The Meaning of Life

What is the meaning of life? How to live to the height of one's potentialities? Life is the dynamic flow of creative joy in the heart of existence. It is the creative adventure of the One seeking to manifest itself in the many; and of the Eternal seeking to manifest itself in time; and of the Infinite seeking to manifest itself in the finite; and of the indivisible Spirit seeking to manifest itself in the endless divisions of matter. As the infinite seeks to manifest itself in the finite, the finite responds to the impact of the infinite with a constant yearning for the Beyond. As the eternal seeks to descend into the flux of time, the individual responds with an aspiration to transcend the limitations of time. Life is thus a constant interaction between the opposite poles of existence. It is a perpetual balancing between apparently contradictory forces. When the balance is disturbed, one is either buried in the material values of time, or shoots up into the ethereal region of the timeless, losing contact with the *terra firma* or solid ground. It is important to discover the bond of connection between the inner aspiration for the Beyond and the creative orientation toward the here-and-now. It is important to discover the golden thread between the ascending movement of the finite and the descending movement of the infinite. The full flowering of life depends upon the discovery of that golden thread.

The creative fulfillment of life depends upon a balanced integration of such seemingly conflicting aspects of existence as the material and the spiritual, the external and the internal, the individual and the universal. In harmonious self-development one has to take proper care of the body, not just for the sake of the body, but as a medium of manifestation of the higher spiritual nature. Similarly, one has more and more to realize the inner self, not with a view to escaping from the burden of material existence, but in order to manifest the glories of the spirit in the material medium. Then again, it is desirable that every individual should be able to grow from within, following the bent of his own nature and the indications of his own psychical make-up, with a view to the full flowering of his unique potentialities. But the balance of life is disturbed when such constructive self-development assumes the form of arrogant and aggressive self-assertion. The unfoldment of individuality is intended to be a unique center of self-expression of the cosmic whole. Every individual has therefore to realize that with all his uniqueness and creative potentialities he is part and parcel of one universal life. Realization of the universal aspect of existence is necessary to give right perspective to one's vision, right direction to one's effort, and right application to one's talent. If experience of the unique produces creative power, experience of the cosmic produces wisdom and love. The secret of happiness lies in a creative fusion of the unique and the cosmic.

The Meaning of God

What is the truth about God? Is God like an almighty great great grandfather, with white beard and flowing garments, seated on a golden throne in the high heavens, and ruling the vast universe with flashes of his eye-signals? That is how popular imagination has it. It is the projection on to the cosmic plane of the father image in the collective unconscious of man. It is the anthropomorphic Deity of popular theism,—the Deity created in the image of man. If a lion were to think of God, he would have visualized God as an all-powerful cosmic Lion controlling the whole world with his mighty paws. Likewise, an elephant, given some imagination, would have fancied God as a sky-high elephant ruling the stars and the planets with his powerful trunk. The truth is we have to go beyond such fanciful forms and projections of wishful thinking in our search for the supreme reality. God is the cosmic creative principle which is the source of all existence, and which imparts meaning to life and to the world process. In essence God is impersonal and indefinable, beyond the limits of human imagination, and baffling to the verbal resources of the human intellect. A satisfactory way in which we may try to make clear to our mind the nature of the logically indefinable cosmic principle which we call God will be somewhat as follows:

In our attempt to understand the nature and existence of anything, say a watch or a building, we inquire into different factors that have gone into its making. First we inquire into the material cause (*upādāna kārana*) or the substance of which it is made. In the case of the building, it may be the bricks and mortar and cement. Then we have to consider the manual skill and labor that have been required to construct the building. This is the efficient cause (*nimitta kārana*). Then we have to take into account the design or the model of which the building is the material embodiment. This design first existed in the mind of the architect or the engineer before it could be given embodiment through right arrangement of the appropriate material. This is the formal cause (*vijñāna*). Finally, we want to know the reason or purpose for the construction of the building. Everything else depends upon this purpose. If the building had been intended to be a school house, then there would be one kind of design; if it had been intended to be a small or large residential house, then there would be another kind of design; if it had been intended to be a church or temple, then there would be another kind of design. The purpose implies the pleasure or satisfaction of those for whom the building is constructed. This is the final cause (*ānanda*). It is the interrelation of these four factors, the material, efficient, formal and final causes (*sat, shakti, vijñāna* and *ānanda*) which throws full light upon the existence and nature of everything.

In human creation we often find these four cause-factors in varying degrees separate from each other. But it is not difficult for us to imagine them existing as inseparable aspects of the same reality. God as the ultimate unifying principle of the universe is the unity of these four factors. God as the material cause of the world is the one infinite substance of which all things and beings are made. But the nature of that substance is pure consciousness (*cit*). God is thus the one cosmic consciousness or ideation which provides the material for all the multitudinous forms of existence in the world. All the realities of the actual world are made of the stuff of divine consciousness, just as our dream-objects are made of the stuff of human unconscious, or just as all the events and characters of a drama are made of the experience and creative imagination of the dramatist. God is in this respect a cosmic dreamer (*Hiranyagarbha*) or the supreme artist or poet. Needless to say, this cosmic consciousness is essentially different from the rational consciousness of the human mind. Such polarities of human experience as conscious and unconscious, personal and impersonal, subject and object, knower and knowable, etc. are the outcome of the self-differentiating power of the same cosmic consciousness which is God. This brings us to the truth that God is also the efficient cause of the world. In the case of the building of our illustration, the masons who build it are existentially different from the bricks, mortar, cement, etc. out of which they build it. But in God the creative energy and the material substance are united. God is cosmic energy (*shakti*),—the dynamism of cosmic consciousness,—of which physical energy, life force, mental power, etc. are different forms of manifestation. As the formal cause or the ordering principle,—the principle which is responsible for transforming chaos into cosmos and for creating order and harmony in accordance with archetypal models,— God is cosmic intelligence or absolute idea (*vijñāna* in Sanskrit, and *nous* in Greek). God is the Idea of all ideas,—the creative intelligence from which all archetypal patterns or formative principles of the world

(10)

proceed, giving rise to things of beauty and sublimity. As the final cause of the world, God is cosmic delight or universal love. In the case of the building, the purpose is external to the material of which it is made, and may also be external to the masons and the architect. But in the case of the world the purpose is inherent in the world process; it is internal to the creative power. The purpose of world-creation is no desire or wish in the human sense of the word, because that would imply imperfection in the infinite creator. It is a kind of purposeless purpose, unmotivated and unfettered self-expression. The best analogue we have of that in our human experience is play, love or esthetic creation. When a child plays, he plays wholeheartedly and spontaneously, without any reserve or ulterior motive in his mind. When a man is in genuine love, he does things and makes all kinds of sacrifice just for the sake of love and with no extraneous motive. In pure esthetic creation, the artist pours himself out freely and spontaneously just for the joy of it. God is the purpose and reason of the world in this sense. The divine purpose of creation is the free self-expression of creative joy, the self-manifestation of the supreme spirit in different media and in different rhythms. It is the creative adventure of the spirit in the apparent contraries of its nature. It is the esthetic urge of the infinite to manifest itself in the finite, the urge of the eternal to manifest itself in time, the urge of the indeterminable to manifest itself in endless determinations.

It is not to be understood from the above that life is no serious affair, or that there are not flaws in life, or that there is no suffering in the world. A game is spoiled if the rules of the game are not scrupulously followed, and if there are not changing fortunes of victory and defeat, loss and gain, joy and sorrow. The cosmic drama is certainly compounded of pains and pleasures, tears and laughter, tragedies and comedies, that are consequential to the operation of universal laws. Only, these laws are not externally imposed upon the creator, but are self-imposed in the best interests of creative self-expression. The tragedies and comedies of life are inseparable moments in the objective realization of creative joy and love. The more we comprehend this profound truth, the more we are liberated from the terrific tensions of existence and can participate in life in a spirit of free and joyful affirmation. To realize God as love is not to deny the existence of suffering and of tragedy, but to transmute them into spiritual bliss. To realize God as delight is not to become passive and indrawn, but to tap the deepest springs of action and to live richly and abundantly without any reserve or fear or inner conflict.

We are now in a position to sum up the nature of God, the supreme Truth, by saying that God is cosmic consciousness (*cit*), cosmic energy (*shakti*), cosmic intelligence (*vijñāna*) and cosmic delight or universal love (*ānanda* or *prema*). God is the universal creative principle of which consciousness, energy, intelligence and love are inseparable aspects.

The Voice of Silence

It is in the depth of silence
    that heaven's deep voice is heard;
'Tis in the soul's sanctuary
    that the wholesome vision is stirr'd.

It is when one calmly withdraws
    into the heart's inner chamber,
That the divine purpose of life
    is unerringly remember'd.

'Tis when the mind stops chattering,
    and the drive of desire is spent,
That the voice of silence speaketh,
    the will of the Divine is felt.

'Tis when the ego makes a sacrifice
    at the altar of the eternal,
That you feel the thrilling transforming touch
    of the radiant light supernal.

'Tis when the intellect renounces
    its conceit and vain pretensions,
That groping in darkness is replaced
    by direct supramental vision.

'Tis when all cravings and ambitions
    are swallowed up in one divine passion,
That the fort of ignorance is storm'd,
    and regained is the kingdom of heaven.

The Secret of Meditation

Meditation is the mind's self-relating to the infinite;
It is the joining of the conscious surface
    to the subliminal depth of the spirit.
Meditation is the technique of complete self-
    integration;
It is the art of self-unfolding,
    a psychological re-orientation.
Meditation is the means of discovering
    the unique rhythm of one's being;
In accord with one's own peculiar talent,
    'tis progressive developing.

Meditation is gathering the power of silence:
    When silence settles in the mind,
        perfect peace holds sway;
    When the heart is filled with love,
        all doubts are cast away;
    Then is set the stage
    For the play of divine grace.

Meditation is searching self-examination:
    When all prejudices are rooted out,
        all narrowness outgrown;
    When the searching light of self-inquiry
        lights up the unknown;
    Then is opened the door
    To a divine downpour.

Meditation is inward self-purification:
    When the storm of passion blows over,
        the dust of desire subsides;
    When the pure flame of aspiration
        in the midst of darkness shines;
    Then is revealed to the soul
    The supreme truth as a whole.

Meditation is psychological house-cleaning:
    When the mental mirror is cleansed,
        the gloom of despair disappears;
    When the clouds of ignorance disperse,
        uprooting all deep-seated fears;
    Then is reflected in our life,
    The glory of the inner light.

Meditation is psychic self-opening:
    When the budding psychic
        opens to the higher;
    When the spirit of love
        blossoms like a flower;
    Then is brought into play
    The supra-mental ray.

Meditation is unreserv'd self-offering:
    When the mental makes an offering
        to the vision supra-mental;
    When the vital goes through suffering
        out of love for the eternal;
    When the physical gladly submits
        to the rigors of the ideal;
    Then is struck the right hour
    For inner life to flower.

Self-Offering

May our whole life be unto Thee
    a supreme act of self-offering,
As the burning flame gives out light,
    through continuous self-consuming.

May all our actions be performed
    for the sake of Thy glory;
May all our thoughts be centered
    on Thy ultimate victory.

May all our feelings and impulses,
    desires and wishful thinking,
Be swallow'd up entire and transform'd
    into one Godward yearning.

May all our endless strife and struggle,
    and passions uncontrollable,
Be transcended and sublimated,
    and made for Thee serviceable.

May all wrong movements of our nature,
    wrong feelings, wishes and thoughts,
Be ruthlessly eliminated,
    and a total purging wrought.

May all our idle curiosities,
    and loud arrogant pretensions,
Be hushed up into humility,
    for Thy gracious revelation.

May all our senseless vanities,
    and shameless self-assertion,
Be shamed into the right spirit
    of willing self-donation.

May all our worries and anxieties,
    and countless calculations,
Be engulfed in the living moment's
    rich, momentous fruition.

The Awful Void

The supreme truth is indeterminable;
Its inner riches inexhaustible.

Baffling the human intellect,
Exceeding logical notions,
Outsoaring all rigid concepts,
And proud verbalized expressions,
    The truth shines by intrinsic light.
Resolving all inner conflicts,
Harmonizing contradictions,
Settling endless verbal disputes,
And dissolving inward tensions,
    The truth is revealed, pure and bright.

Truth is experience ineffable;
Its latent mystery unfathomable.

Transcending all scriptures,
Breaking the pride of learning,
Silencing all strictures
In theological wrangling,
    The truth reigns as the awful void.
Amazing to the intellect,
Attractive to the awaken'd soul,
Irresistible to the heart
As our life's ultimate goal,
    The truth is the supreme beloved.

The Dance of Shiva

Shiva's dance is cosmic rhythm,
The dance of creative joy
That overflows into life's manifold richness.
As Shiva dances in thrill'd ecstasy,
Worlds are created and destroyed.
Suns, moons, stars, and planets,
Are kept unswerving in their courses.
Daily ushered into existence are myriads of living atoms,
And daily disappear millions into non-being.
The vibrating life-impulse advances;
Through changing phases it grows and then decays.
From form to form leaps forward the creative spark,
Until it mingles in the central splendor.

Shiva's dance is enchanting magic.
It spreads in widening circles
Throughout the expanding universe.
Those who are inwardly open
Catch the magic influence.
And lo! shattered are all their evil dreams,
Broken to pieces their self-made fetters.
Old crutches and coverings all outgrown,
They find life a joint enterprise of man and God,
A partnership in the dance of pure delight.

Shiva's dance is all-devouring flame!
It consumes all darkness and gloom,
And reduces to ashes all self-deluded ugliness.
Shiva dances in the crematorium,
Where death brings down to the same level
All distinctions of high and low, rich and poor;
Where the flesh is consigned to the flames,
And turned into a transparent veil of the undying spirit;
Where passions cool down in contact with the raging
        fires.

As Shiva dances with death and terror in his hands,
It evokes a response in the heroic heart.
Out of the ruins of all fixed forms
Is born a new life of imperishable effulgence,—
A life of which death is the pedestal,
And love the crowning jewel.

Life

Life is the self-painting of the spirit
    On the canvas of time and space,—
Gradual unveiling of the infinite
    In Nature's sweet silent embrace.

On the limitless expanse of the ocean
Life is the rising roaring undulation;
On the bosom of the absolute void,
It is the outburst of joy unalloy'd.
In the heart of all-encompassing darkness,
It is the sure conquest of light in harness;
Right in the midst of chaotic disorder,
'Tis the principle of harmony and order.

Life is the play of hide and seek
    Between Spirit and Nature;
Spirit hiding in a deep dark veil,
    Nature tries it to discover.
As Nature moves forward in pursuit
    of Spirit's hidden treasure,
Life leaps forth into radiant glory
    In ever increasing measure.

The Mystic Word

At the beginning was awful silence;
Bubbled from its depth mighty eloquence,—
The all-pervading mystic word,
That contained the seed of the world.
The divine word assumed the entrancing form
Of celestial music, the resounding AUM.
As cosmic vibration, spreading far and wide,
It brought into being the cosmic tide.

The starry heavens above,
The noisy world below,
The free-moving gods above,
Struggling multitudes below,
     All sprang from the same music;
The stern moral law within,
March of vanity without,
The sovereign light within,
Mad unceasing search without,
     Are varied notes authentic.

The mystic word is indeed the foundation
Of the boundless multi-color'd creation.
As the triune truth of the original,
It utters forth elements essential.
Creation, maintenance, and dissolution,
Are intertwin'd aspects of evolution.
Existence, knowledge and supreme delight,
In the essence of the spirit unite.
Mind, life-force, and unconscious matter,
Are component factors of nature.
Waking, dream, and death-like sleep dreamless,
Are three forms of the same consciousness.

But all this triple manifestation
Is embraced in the creative vision
Of the same unmanifest unity
That shines in unruffl'd serenity.

The Dance of Kāli

The dance of Kāli is the unfoldment of the cosmic drama
Against the background of timeless perfection.
It is the unceasing march of time
Against the background of eternity.
It is the irresistible onrush of the creative urge
On the basis of timeless freedom.
Kāli dances on the bosom of Shiva,—
The dance of dark deep energy
Flowing from wisdom's white radiance,—
The dance of clouds with lightning flashes
In the boundless vault of the heavens.

The dance of Kāli is quick disillusionment;
It is the breaking of all bonds,
And the tearing of distorting veils.
It is the act of piercing with a swift stroke
Centuries of darkness slowly accumulated.
It is the act of unmasking abysmal ignorance
And ruthless shattering of its silvery filaments.
It is the act of charming the master charmer,
And dehypnotizing the hypnotiz'd soul.
Kāli's dance is divine intoxication.
To everything ignoble and mean,
It spells absolute rack and ruin.

Nirvāna

Is Nirvāna the heaven of popular fancy, where no wish
  is left unfulfill'd?
Is it the enchanted land of lotus-eating, that satisfies
  all human greed?

Nirvāna is in fact the discovery of pure delight beyond
  all desire;
It is the abode of truth and beauty, built upon love's
  all-consuming fire.

Is Nirvāna the heaven of nothingness, the abysmal pit
  of non-being?
Is it the peace of total extinction, the joy of self-
  annihilating?

Nirvāna is spiritual enlightenment, beyond the reach
  of logical notions;
'Tis the state of perfect tranquility, beyond emotional
  fluctuations.

Nirvāna is pure transcendental peace, beyond all psychic
  polarities;
It is living in harmony with eternal spiritual verities.

It is being beyond birth and death, vision beyond truth
  and error;
Perfection beyond right and wrong, bliss beyond all
  pain and pleasure.

Nirvāna is ineffable experience, liquidating ignorance
  and ego,
Transcending the self and the non-self, and ceaseless
  changes of the cosmic flow.

Is Nirvāna the end of all action, a fearful escape from
    life?
Is it a farewell to life's duties, and a lonely mystic flight?

Nirvāna is in essence the secret of non-action in action;
Of a spontaneous active life it is the firm foundation.

Negation that is involved in Nirvāna is only a step to
    deeper affirmation;
An aid to mind's re-orientation, and a factor in a higher
    transformation.

Nirvāna is in essence the harmony of wisdom, love and
    tranquility,—
Re-valuation of all life's values, in the light of divine
    unity.

Thy Name is Wisdom

O the supreme mystery, unfathomable in essence!
Thou art visible only to the soul's inward eye,
For thy name is wisdom.

(Thou art) Wisdom in social development,
    Wisdom in cultural unfoldment:
    Wisdom that forgives the hand that crucifies,
    Wisdom that tolerates the tongue that vilifies,
    Wisdom that reveals the grandeur of truth,
    Wisdom that teaches the unity of all being,
    Wisdom that fights universal freedom to win,
    Wisdom that sees pervading all existence
    One all-fulfilling spiritual essence.

The Kingdom of Heaven

Is the kingdom of heaven without or within? Is it above
    or inside the material?
Is it a reality verifiable? Or just an imaginary ideal?

In essence it is experience ineffable, beyond all relations
    and distinctions;
Where without, within, above and inside, are all
    meaningless expressions.

It is the abode of absolute truth, beyond both existence
    and non-existence;
Beyond all conceptual differences, and the conflicting
    verdicts of sense.

As it transcends all distinctions, it also embraces them
    all;
'Tis indeed the light of all lights, where all jarring
    discords dissolve.

The kingdom of heaven is within, for God is the inner
    controller,
The Secret truth of all existence, every being's
    indwelling ruler.

The kingdom of heaven is above, not indeed in point of
    space or matter,
But as higher planes of consciousness, interpenetrating
    one another.

The kingdom of heaven is without; for the world
    stretching before our eyes,
Is, in truth, a rhythmic expression of the creative joy
    which in God resides.

The kingdom of heaven is ahead; for, through perpetual
	evolution,
The birth of an ever-new order is artful Nature's creative
	mission.

The kingdom of heaven is here and now; for, the
	timeless essence of our being
Is the fullness of pure joy that transcends the chance and
	change of ceaseless becoming.

Thy Name is Peace

O the nameless Transcendence,
Thy name is peace,
Peace within and peace without;
Peace above in the boundless blue,
Peace below in friendliness true;
Peace in the galaxy of shining stars,
Peace in the happiness of singing birds.

Peace in the ocean's endless expanse,
Peace in the lover's thrilling romance.
Peace in the summits of mute mountains,
Peace in the freshness of running fountains.
Peace in the wonders of the world of sense,
Peace in the depths of human experience.

Peace in the sphere of unceasing action,
Peace in quiet and relax'd contemplation;
Peace in the travail of new creation,
Peace in death and cyclic dissolution.
Peace in the midst of struggling nations,
Peace in the march of civilization!

Unity

Life's essence is unity,
God is the name they give it:
Unity that makes the whole of existence one unbroken
  continuum;
Unity that claims for all human races the same precious
  right to freedom.

The different streams of human culture merge in a grand
  harmony;
Mutually enriching one another they are all one in many.

The different religions of the world are all varied notes
  of one symphony;
They all emphasize devotion to truth as the one cure of
  human agony.

The diverse currents of philosophic thinking are blended
  in Truth's immediate presence;
They are varied modes of self-articulation of the one
  non-dual supramental essence.

The different standards of human action, ideologies
  seemingly conflicting,
Harmonize in purpose of evolution, in the common need
  of collective living.

With a true change of man's inner nature, with
  enlighten'd self-interest in sway,
All obstacles to enduring human peace are bound in a
  trice to melt away.

Unity is no colorless uniformity, no regimentation of life
and thought;
No imposition of one identical pattern with devilish,
heartless compulsion wrought.

It is the play of endless variations flowing from the same
boundless source,—
A fusion of countless multiplicity, a harmony of diverse
notes.

Identity

The enchantment that spreads in the starry heavens
above
Is akin to the joy that throbs in the depth of human love.

The marvelous power that wells up in the endless variety
of nature
Is attuned to the increasing purpose that runs through the
historical order.

The mystery that reveals itself through the immensities
of time and space
Is akin to the small inner voice that lends to human life
its charm and grace.

The voice that solemnly speaks through terrific storm
and thunder
Is also the spirit that breathes in the dancing streamlet's
murmur.

The impulse that occasionally breaks forth in war's
destructive fury
Is the same as builds up through sublimation the soul's
constructive glory.

Know Thyself

The profound word of wisdom that rings through the
    ages,
Declares unambiguously one supreme message:
Know the secret of thy self, thy own inmost centre;
Discover in thy inner temple, the world's greatest
    wonder.
In one tiny atom is reflected the whole of matter;
In one negligible drop is hidden the mystery of all water;
In a single leaf of the tree is outlined its unique pattern;
In a single line of a book is contained its special design,
So also in every finite soul dwells the infinite supreme;
In the inmost recess of the heart shines the eternal
    undimm'd.

To know the secret of the self is the master key to
    possess
To unlock the mysteries of being with sovereign ease
    and success.
To discover the Self of self is the master light to attain,
That dispels all darkness and doubt the lost harmony to
    regain.

Deeper than intellect and ego, the Self is the principle of
    unity;
Connecting man with man, each with all, 'tis the bond of
    universality.
Deeper than the conscious and unconscious, the Self is
    the centre superconscious;
Uniting man with God, part with the whole, it is the
    infinite's unique focus.
To know the Self is to discover the individual's unique
    mission,—
The purpose of the Divine in life, and the secret of final
    fruition.

The Playful Mystery

God is an eternal child playing in an eternal garden,
Making infinite designs, constantly unmaking them
    again.
There is no purpose in creation, except the expression of
    creative delight,—
Play of infinite variations that in the same unbroken
    thread of life unite.

The child plays on the seashore, casting and re-casting
    grains of sand;
Creation is an ever-shifting scene of novelties fresh and
    brand.

The growing movement of our life, the evolutionary
    advance of nature,
Is in the dark depth of matter, the Spirit's creative
    adventure.
The three periods of time are simultaneously present
In one flash of intuition to the supreme superconscient.

God is called the Father, the creative light everlasting;
Perfect wisdom that holds the cycle of life revolving.

God is called the Mother, the universal force of life;
Pure all-embracing love from which all cosmic forms
    derive.
God is the eternal Comrade, the unfailing friend in need;
The inner guide that renders help regardless of caste and
    creed.

God is the perfect Mate of man's loving heart;
Sweet bridegroom to the soul that plays the bridal part.

God is the great Silence that no words can ever reach;
The infinite awful void that is infinitely rich.

Truth is Bipolar

That which is spaceless and timeless in space and time is
    self-extended;
Space provides the silent background where time's
    creation is unfolded.

That which is beyond mind and matter in matter and
    mind is self-expressed;
Matter provides the firm foundation, where mental
    fabrics are erected.

That which is neither subject nor object into two poles is
    bifurcated;
The objective is the changing many which in the subject
    is united.

That which is beyond spirit and nature in a twofold
    structure is divided;
Nature is the nurse of all existence, spirit is inward
    vision undistracted.

That which is neither male nor female in a dual form is
    manifested;
The male is the unmoved onlooker, for whom the cosmic
    dance is enacted.

That which is beyond all verbalized expression, as a
    harmony of contrasts is reveal'd;
As at once the daunting and the fascinating, which is a
    tremendous mystery indeed.

That which is beyond all determinations, as a unity of
    opposites is express'd;
As at once the merciful and the terrible, for whom
    feelings of love and awe are blended.

That which is beyond all movement in time as the stream
    of becoming is manifested;
Where, from the ruins of running destruction, novel
    forms and patterns are ever constructed.

That which is pure ineffable experience, as the cosmic
    mind is articulated;
Of which the content is the whole universe, and the
    centre is everywhere located.

Affirmation

I affirm my faith in the unity of all mankind,
In the meeting of diverse races in one cosmic mind.
I affirm my faith in the universality of light,
Whose eternal music breaks into the glory of life.

I affirm my faith in the dignity of man,
And his significant place in the cosmic plan.
I affirm my faith in the Divine in history;
In right's superior might and eventual victory.

I affirm my faith in our life's profound meaning,
In the rich splendor of its gradual blossoming.
I affirm my faith in the harmony of human culture,
In the emergence of a stable international structure.
I affirm my faith in the most fruitful meeting of East and
    West,
In the untold blessings that on peaceful cooperation rest.

I affirm my faith in love's limitless power,
Which alone can bring the grace of God in shower;
Which can turn life into a poem of pure delight,
And bring the reign of abiding peace into sight;
Which can turn evil into good and conquer fear,
And transform opposition into friendship rare.

Two in One

Reality is two in one, one in two,—
Timeless eternity and ceaseless flux of time,
Nameless mystery and nature's creative flow.
The two are no separate spheres of being,
The one excluding or canceling the other.
They intertwine and interpenetrate,
And are inseparable dimensions of the same life.
The formless bursts forth in endless forms
Which spread their charms, hold the stage,
And are re-absorbed in the fathomless void.

Man as a living image of that mystery
Is a citizen of two worlds
By birth and by reason of destiny.
His self-fulfillment lies in increasing awareness
Of this dual citizenship.
The soul is his rootedness
In full freedom of the void.
The mind is his passport
To the wondrous world of multi-colored forms.
By meditation he realizes more and more
The inward freedom which is boundless.
By action he participates more and more
In the creative flow of life which is endless.
By love of God and love of man,
By total self-transcendence in divine delight,
By integral self-offering to that central flame of
        existence,
Which is being's perpetual self-becoming,
He links up meditation with action,
Expressing freedom in the sphere of bondage,
And manifesting the one in the sphere of the many.

The Religion of Man

Religion above all religions is the religion of man,
The religion of peace and progress, and of one cosmic
    plan.

To strive for unity of races, to bring them all together;
To unite all discordant forces in collective endeavor;
To expunge hatred and violence, one exploiting another;
To stop aggression and expansion, at the cost of the
    neighbor;
Is the noblest religious effort that man can ever make,—
The crowning glory of our life without doubt or mistake.

To replace violence with love as the ruling principle of
    life;
To champion freedom for all for which devoutly to
    strive;
To renounce the self for service as the one absorbing
    pastime;
To affirm the presence in all of one universal divine;
Is the noblest act of faith of which man is ever capable,
The deepest vision of truth, the finest spirit adorable.

To strive for social equality, uniting rich and poor;
To hold up the ideal of justice, to all an open door;
To embrace all in friendliness, in warm cordiality;
To assist all to manifest their latent divinity;
Is the noblest form of worship that man can conceive;—
The highest form of fulfillment that one can achieve.

Trinity

God is one without a second, an indivisible unity;
Yet He has interwov'n aspects: a significant trinity.

As a principle of unity, He is not a featureless blank,
But a rich source of variety of various power and rank.

As an opulent trinity, He has three different aspects,
Three basic modes of existence, three clearly discernible
facets.

As the ultimate source of the world, He is the creative
universal;
As the deep mystery unfathomable, He is the ineffable
transcendental.

But the same infinite reality, that creatively sustains the
many,
Is also present in every unit as profound principle of
harmony.

Reality as God the Father is the peace that passeth the
understanding;
And the same conceived as God the Son is the creative
logos life-sustaining.

Again, the same rich Personality who is unity of love
and peace,
Does also dwell in the individual as the potent spark of
divine bliss.

God the Holy Ghost is no other than the spark of the
Divine in the finite;
He gives to every living creature to the kingdom of
heaven his divine right.

In the intrinsic nature of God are three essential
     elements:
Existence, consciousness and delight, which are no
     separable fragments.

In the dynamic nature of God are three closely
     interwoven functions;
As related to the world they are creation, maintenance
     and dissolution.

In a logical analysis of God are three interrelated
     moments;
Idea, nature and infinite spirit, three basic logical
     components.

Idea is objective thought, the subsistent universal;
Nature is the cosmic flux, the sphere of the particular.

Spirit is the identity, in which idea and nature
Meet together in harmony and in perfect composure.

In a psychological approach to God, are three essential
     factors:
Subject, object and the indefinable void, interwov'n in
     psychic texture.

God is the absolute non-being, the silence of the
     superconscious,
In which subject and object meet in an experience
     harmonious.

God as Love

The Supreme is more than the cosmic lover,
More than the infinite beloved power,
More than the magic bond that binds together.

It is the inclusive whole
Reveal'd in the depth of soul
    as lover, loving, lovable;
'Tis the ineffable unity
Self-expressed in the trinity
    of knower, knowing, knowable.

God as love is responsive
To man's loving offensive
    of worship, meditation, and prayer;
To bless him with perfect grace,
To hold him in sweet embrace,
    He is ever patiently eager.

God as love chooses to stay,
Renouncing the royal way,
    in the humble cottage of the faithful;
Rejecting the pomp of the crown,
He hastens to the downtrodden,
    to accept their offerings, a handful.

God as love is gentle persuasion
A hater of violent coercion,
    with infinite patience to wait;
He enters the heart of the simple,
Turns it into a divine temple,
    when man gladly opens the gate.

God as love is joy creative,
Eternal urge self-expansive,
    that pours out in infinite variations;
He is the flame that never flickers,
The compassion that never wavers,
    the kind purpose that runs through all creations.

Negation and Affirmation

God is the highest limit of all negation,
And also the basis of all affirmation.

Negating unconscious matter,
Negating the subconscious life,
Negating the self-conscious mind,
And the superconscious spirit,
    God is the supreme unknowable!
Exceeding sensuous intuition,
Exceeding rational understanding,
Exceeding mystic illumination,
And dialectical reasoning,
    God is experience ineffable.

(Yet) Self-expressed as the material,
    Self-expressed as vital power,
    Self-expressed as the pure mental,
    And modes of being still higher,
        God is infinite creativity;
    Self-articulating through the senses,
    And through clear-cut logical thinking,
    Self-revealing through aesthetic images,
    And through intuitive apprehending,
        God is the all-affirming unity.

Male and Female

The Real in its inmost essence is beyond all distinction;
It knows no difference in sex, no internal division.

It can hardly be regarded as heavenly father or mother;
Neither male nor female is God, neither sister nor
    brother.

Indeterminable in inmost essence, but still, in cosmic
    expression,
God is the ultimate root and basis of all differentiation.

God is at once the archetypal male, and the female
    archetypal;
Unity of all polar opposites, and their basic truth eternal.

As cosmic male, He is timeless perfection, the white
    radiance of Shiva;
As cosmic female, endless self-expression, Shakti in her
    dynamic flow.

As cosmic male, He is immutable being, Purusa's
    perfect composure;
As cosmic female, mutable becoming, Prakriti's creative
    pleasure.

As cosmic male, He is eternal fact, eternally self-
    accomplished;
As cosmic female, perpetual act, without any goal to be
    reached.

As cosmic male, He is the pure universal, philosophers
    call subsistence;
As cosmic female, the concrete particular, philosophers
    call existence.

As cosmic male, He is absolute thought, the pure infinite
     logos;
As cosmic female, all-embracing love, the all-sustaining
     eros.

As cosmic male, He is infinite wisdom, the pure original
     light;
As cosmic female, self-expansive delight, the one
     universal life.

The Supreme Mystery

Beyond all forms in essence thou art, still self-expressed
     in endless forms;
Beyond all names in essence thou art, still called by
     sages by different names.

Powers, qualities, and attributes are external to thy
     inmost essence;
Still as the source of all determinations thou art the
     centre of the world of sense.

Words and ideas and theories can hardly grasp the
     mystery of thy being;
Still, ever renewed, they are useful aids as a push to our
     life's evolving.

Beyond limits, cosmic and individual, thou art in essence
     absolute freedom;
But still amidst limitations self-imposed, is built thy
     shining limitless kingdom.

Inner Freedom

Independent thinking, unblock'd and undaunted,
Is the key to synoptic vision unclouded.
It opens up vistas, magnificent and bold;
And prepares the mind for wonders untold.

When the shackles of authority are shaken loose,
When tradition's beaten track one ceases to choose;
When the bonds of inertia break, habit's chains drop,
When one leaps forward in joy without any prop;
Then is the truth revealed in native splendor,
And one's entire life is clothed in new grandeur.

Emotional freedom, uncramp'd, unattach'd,
Is the tower of inner strength unmeasur'd.
It opens up the springs of creative living,
And proves in human relations a rare blessing.

Attachment to life's passing phases,
Clinging to changing circumstances,
Wild lamenting for the dead and gone,
Senseless craving for the yet-unborn,
Are the chains that bind the growing soul,
And play in our lives a tragic role.

Unruffl'd calmness of the mind and emotional stability,
Unflinching devotion of the heart and mental equality,
Are conditions essential for spiritual freedom
And the soul's fine flowering in flawless medium.

When idols of the mind are broken,
Rigid dogmas and creeds forsaken;
When shadows of doubt are chased away,
And a flaming faith is holding sway,
Then is the time for the inner voice
To reveal the purpose of life's voyage.

The Deathless Spark

Immortal is the human soul, unborn and undying;
Birth and death are accidents of its upward evolving.

Imperishable is the spirit, undaunted, unyielding;
Regardless of storm and fire, it keeps on ascending.

Dangers may come its way, obstacles without number;
The spirit is sure to triumph, once awaken'd from
    slumber.

Dazzling temptations may distract, dark forces interfere;
Nothing can prevail in the end against the formless fire.

The strength of the soul lies in its rootedness in the
    eternal;
It is the focalized power of the concrete universal.

Child of the infinite, the soul moves forward with
    confidence,
To fulfill its birthright to be reborn in superconscience.

Dynamic centre of the infinite, the soul evolves through
    changing phases;
To express in an increasing measure the inexhaustible
    inner riches.

Growing image of the eternal, the soul shines undimm'd,
To transform the world around us into an abode of Truth
    unveil'd.

Involved in a cosmic adventure in the depth of the
    inconscient,
The soul aims to express in matter glories of the
    superconscient.

Avatāra or Divine Incarnation

Whenever there is a crisis in cosmic affairs, an eclipse of
the higher values of life,
We witness a special manifestation of God, an
expression of the eternal in time.

The crisis may assume the form of a transition in
civilization;
Then is the time for God's descent in the shape of a
special Incarnation.

Buddha, Lao-tzu, Christ and Confucius, Lord Krishna,
Rāmchandra, and Zoroaster,
Are instances of divine descension in man's
evolutionary endeavor.

Moses, Mohammed, Shankar, and Gāndhi, Rāmkrishna
and Aurobindo,
Are instances of the non-temporal self-revealed in
history's flow.

Wisdom, love, universal law, intuition, overmind, and
supermind,
Are aspects and powers of truth, actively emphasized at
different times.

Beauty, beatitude and harmony, peace, freedom and
unity,
Are diverse elements of the Divine, dynamized in
society.

The crisis in life may also relate to the inner being of the
individual;
Then is the time for God's revelation as the inner
command or light internal.

It is indeed in the thick of darkness that the great Avatāra
 is born;
When everything seems quite lost all around, everything
 is set right again.

Whenever the evolving individual truly transcends the
 ego,
The universal is born in his consciousness in all its
 majestic glow.

The Many in One

Different rivers flow into the same vast ocean;
Different flowers bloom in the same spacious garden;
Different branches spread from the same strong stem;
Different sparks fly from the same burning flame;
So also the divergent religious systems of the world,
Are various expressions of the same unfathomable
 Word.

The infinitely diverse streams of philosophic thinking,
Of the same multiform truth are varied modes of
 conceiving.
The endless plurality of unique individual beings,
From one common source of life, dance out in deep joy
 like springs.
The multi-colored races in different parts of the globe,
Of the same human glory are various pillars of hope.
The many-branching currents of man's growing culture,
Flow from the same rich spirit's creative adventure.

The Superman

The superman is the promise of human nature,
The secret urge of nature's creative advance,
The hidden significance of the unfolding history
Of man's inner contradictions and incomplete triumphs.
The superman is the dynamics of man's growing
    consciousness,
The bursting forth of the inner spirit
From its adventurous plunge in the dark abyss.

The superman is not the outflowering of the ego,
Not the titanic over-growth, not the lopsided monster,
That seeks to assert its supremacy by devouring the
    world.
Nor is supermanhood a special gift from above,
Intended to be the monopoly of a privileged few.

It is the birthright of man as man,
The full flowering of man's inmost nature,
Just as manhood is the mature fruition
Of the growing powers of animal nature.

The superman conquers the world
By his readiness to serve the world through self-
    immolation.
He asserts his inward infinity
By offering himself without reserve at the altar of the
    infinite;
He commands universal love and respect
By his worship of the universal in one and all;
He is immortalized in human hearts
By his glad submission to death as a shadow of the
    eternal.

Supermanhood implies entire transformation of nature
     and consciousness
In the light of that which is beyond both light and
     darkness.
It implies a radical change of the texture and pattern of
     human living,
By bringing into play the supra-mental truth in the flux
     of our becoming;
It implies a complete integration of the different aspects
     of our existence,
A dissolving of inner conflicts and discords in an
     outflow of life's deeper essence.

Thy Name is Love

O the ineffable One, inaccessible to thought!
Thou art knowable to love alone,
For thy name is love.
(Thou art) Love in man, woman, and nature,
Love in every living creature;
Love in interatomic attraction,
Love in planetary gravitation;
Love in male and female that attract each other,
Love in the light festival of the moon and stars;
Love in martyrs' willing sacrifice,
Love in mystics' all-embracing eyes;
Love in the glories of sunrise and sunset,
Love in the revealing of nature's secret;
Love in the rhythmic dance of day and night,
Love in kind leading of the inner light.

The Meaning of Life

Is our life an empty dream?
A nightmare that frightens, or a shadow-show that
    passes away?

Is our life an idiot's tale?
A rigmarole that bores, or a magician's illusive sway?

Or, is our life a stern duty?
    An arduous path that knows no end?
Or, is it a thing of multi-colored beauty?
    A marvelous texture of varied blend?

Life is indeed a dream, not empty but real;
It is indeed a tale, not unmeaning, but told so
    magnificently well.
Life is indeed a duty, not a blind alley;
Nor is it a journey without goal, a joyless endless way.

Life is in essence a symphony, with an infinite variety of
    notes intermingl'd;
Seeming discords dissolved in the total, special tunes
    waiting to be disentangl'd.

At the centre is creative joy, love and beauty its
    expressions;
Every moment is life fulfilled, but still always a new
    excursion.

Duty is life's law of fulfillment, and beauty its rhythm of
    unfolding;
Action its mode of self-expression, and bliss eternal its
    stuff of being.

Silence

There is power in silence,—
A power mightier than the aggressive flow of eloquence,
A power born of quiet self-gathering and self-
    confidence,
A power that breaks all self-created trammels,
And works pervasively through invisible channels.
The power of silence is irresistible,
Emanating from the depth
Of a living flaming faith.

There is a truth in silence,—
A truth more illuminating than missionary zeal,
A truth that propagates itself in a spirit tranquil,
Discarding all methods of propaganda,
Spurning the debates over plann'd agenda,
    absorbing and exhausting all superficial thoughts.
The truth of silence is self-luminous,
It is invariably contagious,
Especially when it flows,
From the depth of self-repose.

There is a freedom in silence,—
Freedom from compelling needs of self-expression,
Freedom from the fetters of blind self-assertion,
Freedom from all unmeaning self-dissipation,
And myriad forms of imposed limitation.
The freedom of silence is immaculate;
Born of total transcendence of all rigid forms,
'Tis boundless possibility, measureless norm.

The Flame of Love (Rādhā's Longing)

I

The devoted wife Rādhā
Was minding her household duties,
When suddenly the strange music,
The compelling melody of Krishna's flute,
Reached her ears, ravished her heart,
Made her captive, sound-intoxicated.
She forgot her work in hand,
Forgot her family surroundings.
Suddenly cut adrift from secure moorings,
She set out in search of Krishna.

(This is what happens to the human soul
When one day, at a psychological moment,
Comes the call of the Divine,
Penetrates the inmost being,
Unsettles life's settled order,
Leads with irresistible inner compulsion
Toward the unknown and unseen.)

II

Along rugged pathways strewn with wild thorns,
Through dense forests infested with blood-thirsty beasts,
In darkness made darker with dazzling flashes of
        lightning,
Through angry storms whipping the lethargy of night,
She went on, undaunted, undistracted,
With eyes fixed on one goal.
Her ears filled with the melody of the flute,
Had no room for shrieks of wild ferocity.
All her clothing torn and blasted away one after another,
Her feet bleeding from sharp thorns,
Her slim figure shivering in piercing cold,

She came at last to the spot,
Where Krishna was playing the flute, self-absorb'd.
She kissed his feet in deep devotion,
And Krishna took her up in a sweet embrace.

(This is the soul's ecstatic union with the spirit,
A wondrous illumination that comes at the end
Of a long perilous journey in darkness.)

III

Rādhā was now aware of her rare good fortune,
Aware of her incomparable blessedness.
Her mind loved to dwell on her unique privilege;
Her fancy freely played around
Weaving golden fabrics of rapture;
In her dreams she expatiated
On the demands and counter-demands of love.
Her heightened sense of individuality
Placed her on a high pedestal.
But alas! Suddenly she saw with her eyes open
That Krishna was no more by her side.
He mysteriously disappeared,
Heartlessly leaving Rādhā alone.

IV

Thus began for Rādhā a long period
Of unbearable separation, of mystic death.
Banished from the kingdom of light
She was a misfit in the realm of darkness.
Her friends and relatives, her near and dear ones,
Even her most loving husband
Believed her not, questioned her fidelity.
The agony of separation was doubly enhanced
By all-surrounding suspicion and cruel
    misunderstanding.

She is now completely alone,
The whole world against her, the most beloved one
     gone.
The terrific pressure of this loneliness
Brought about a new psychic upheaval;
Purged her of the last lingering traces
Of vanity, pride, and self-concern.
No more does she care for her own weal and woe.
There is no more desire in her mind
Even for salvation, the highest human aspiration.
There is no more demand, no more self-assertion,
Nor more craving for thrill'd ecstasies.
Enthron'd in calm serenity and imperturbable peace,
Rādhā is now fit to be Krishna's playmate,
Ready to give him a welcome
Most appropriate to the lord of love.

V

Their re-union is a rare consummation,—
The silence of wisdom vibrating
With love's dynamic urge.
As Krishna and Rādhā dance together
In a rhythmic circle of shining effulgence,
New creative forces are generated,
New powerful vibrations that can transform
The face of earth in increasing measure.

(50)

Diversity

Some sing the praise of pure being;
Some pay homage to pure becoming.
Some affirm the truth as eternal fact,
Some conceive it as continuous act.
Some love to worship timeless perfection;
Some glorify unceasing evolution.
Some take delight in static contemplation;
Some are sick without vigorous action.
Some pin their faith on lofty abstraction;
Some are wedded to sensuous perception.
Some are enamored of the highly mystical;
Some insist on the clear-cut logical.
Some tread the path of complete negation;
Some indulge in increasing affirmation.
Multi-colored is indeed human personality;
Multi-form is the richness of ultimate reality.

Creative Action

Truth is freedom, and freedom is joy;
Life is joyful expression of truth in freedom.

Life is the rhythm of light breaking through darkness;
'Tis the dance of spirit in the heart of matter,
The music of silence beneath all surface turmoil,
The drama of the unseen, visible in tears and laughter.

When a glimpse is caught of the formless light,
When the message is heard from the soundless word,
When the path is cleared for the gateless gate,
The cup of life is filled to the brim,
With the ecstasy of creative action.